BANNERS

on *Favorite Bible Verses*

BANNERS
on Favorite Bible Verses

SALLY BECK

Concordia Publishing House

Variations of some of these designs previously appeared in publications from Creative Communications for the Parish, St. Louis, Missouri.

Copyright © 1998 Concordia Publishing House
3558 S. Jefferson Avenue, St. Louis, MO 63118-3968
Manufactured in the United States of America

The purchaser of this product may reproduce the banner patterns as needed for the completion of a project.

1 2 3 4 5 6 7 8 9 10   07 06 05 04 03 02 01 00 99 98

Contents

New Testament Banners

Preface

Something we consider oh-so-familiar sometimes offers new insights when it appears in a new context. Politicians attempt to spruce up old ideas with new rhetoric. Preachers face the challenge weekly of finding fresh ways to present familiar texts. And sometimes difficult-to-understand ideas become easier to grasp if we can *see* what that idea is like. Poets and preachers give us metaphors or word paintings to do just that. Banners—with their interplay of words, bold shapes, symbols, and colors—do this also as they provide new ways to look at words that we have heard many times or provide visual metaphors with fresh understanding for hidden meanings. Because these words and ideas are found in Scripture, the task is infused with new energy. For God's Word is alive, and the Holy Spirit enables the reader to see valuable things in every encounter.

Words and images are a dynamic combination: Posters, book jackets, T-shirts, billboards, and junk mail all vie for our attention. Banners also combine those two powerful elements to enhance our Sunday worship. I hope that these banner designs will "declare to you what we have seen and heard" (1 John 1:3 NRSV), taking inspiration from the rich language of the psalmists, the prophets, the apostles, and the Lord Himself.

The Bible verses for these designs are some of the favorite passages that believers throughout the years have put to heart, remembered fondly from confirmation, recalled in joys and sorrows, written to encourage others, hung by the front door, and posted on the refrigerator. The banner format is just one more place to declare the truths that God has for us. These designs can aid us in our prayer and praise in worship, or, created in smaller sizes, they can become appropriate gifts for fellow believers.

I hope that the designs in this book have other uses as well. Pastors and church secretaries might find them useful for bulletin covers or newsletter clip art. Teachers easily can turn them into bulletin board designs. And anyone can pull out their colored markers or watercolors to create a fast greeting card by adding color to a photocopy on heavy paper. Whatever purposes creative people will find for them, these banner designs are intended to add joy to the journey of faith.

Sally Beck

Introduction

Whether banners have been assembled by accomplished sewers or are the result of preschoolers' cutting and pasting, they stand or hang before us, the body of believers, offering a glimpse of God's truth and enhancing the worship service with their colorful witness.

The variety of colors, forms, shapes, and textures in creation gives evidence to the joy that God knew when He formed the world. And He allows His creatures that same fun when they create. Liturgical art in the banner format can incorporate a variety of materials available to artists, sewers, and craftspeople and still retain the traditions associated with church art. Many of the symbols and suggested colors for the banners in this book are traditional, but the assembly allows you, the bannermaker, much latitude in choosing materials. The box that still has buttons from your grandmother's sewing days, the boxes of fabric scraps that you've saved for all those quilts you were going to make, the ribbons and embroidery floss from completed or abandoned projects, the shiny beads from the broken necklace—these all offer possibilities to the bannermaker.

Beauty in banner design can take many forms. A large part of that beauty is the personal touch that comes from the faith and imagination of the bannermaker. In other words, these designs are only beginnings that invite you, the artist, to dream your own designs. Move the design elements around, use a favorite lettering style instead, put *your* favorite Bible passage with a design that you like. Don't feel bound by the lines on the page.

Many of the construction ideas that accompany each banner are easy to follow and require little time. Some, however, are time consuming and require some advanced needlework or artistic talent. If you are a novice bannermaker, or you are short on time, ignore the more advanced suggestions and assemble the elements with one of the basic cut-and-paste methods. If you are a quilter or painter or artistic in any of a variety of ways, the advanced ideas will stir your creative energies.

May your colorful results be an integrated part of the worship service where the Lord's presence brings banners, singing voices, lighted candles, litanies, stained-glass, homily, confessions, and bread and wine together in a divine and joyful whole.

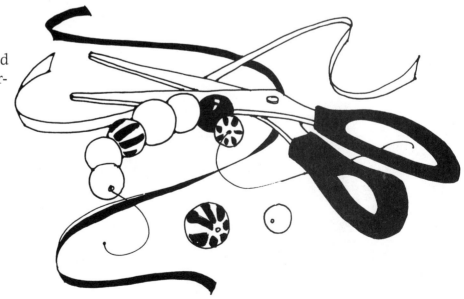

General Directions

Because the individual banner design and its scriptural theme are the determining factors for the choice of materials, the first task of the bannermaker is to spend time mulling over the project, allowing God's Word to warm your creative juices. Let the ideas percolate on a back burner of your mind. Think about the tone of the design: Is it a soft, comforting message? Are the words and design bold and courageous? Should the fabric be flowing? soft and fuzzy? sturdy and unyielding?

Choosing Fabric

After spending time thinking about your banner project, the next step is a trip to the fabric store. Instead of being overwhelmed with options, enjoy the wonderful panoply of colors, textures, patterns, and designs. Indulge your tactile sense. Make your way around the store, touching and holding the various weights of cloth and imagining the background of *your* banner in different colors, weights, and densities of weave.

Think also how the banner will be hung. Does your church have poles for it to be hung from the rafters? Will it be stretched between two poles, or will it be hung from the top of the banner? Will it be carried for processions? Should it move in the breeze of the ceiling fans or from the open doors in summer? Will it hang on a wall? Or will it be a small banner, made for a new baby or as a confirmation gift?

The following fabric descriptions may be helpful. In general, avoid knits and work instead with cottons and cotton blends.

Heavy background fabrics

Cotton Duck—100 percent cotton; bleached or unbleached; 60″ wide; inexpensive.

Heavy felt—72″ wide; variety of colors; reasonably priced.

Heavy Duck—36″ wide; some colors.

Denim—Cotton and blends; 60″ wide; many colors; reasonably priced.

Poplin Plus—60″ wide; beautiful colors; reasonably priced.

Medium-weight background fabrics

Poplin and *Twills*—Cotton and blends; 60″ wide; many colors.

Corduroy—Cotton; 60″ wide; beautiful colors and texture; more expensive.

Linen-Look—Polyester and rayon; 60″ wide; many colors.

Gabardine—Polyester and rayon; 60″ wide; hangs beautifully; more expensive; more difficult to use.

And don't rule out *upholstery* and *drapery fabrics*, which come in a wide variety of beautiful, artistic textures and intriguing weaves. These fabrics vary in price and in ease of handling.

Lightweight background fabric for small banners

Muslin and *Skimmer muslin*—45″ wide; permanent-press type; inexpensive; great for classroom individual banner projects and for a natural look.

Chintz and *Sateen*—Polished cotton; 45″ wide; firm; easy to use.

Heavy-weight interfacing (Pellon brand)—24″ wide; translucent; inexpensive; great for classroom individual projects. (Banner 14 requires this.)

China silk—Beautiful; inexpensive; more difficult to use.

Fabrics for design elements

Sometimes it is desirable for the background fabric and the fabric used for the design pieces to be the same. Any of the background fabrics listed can serve as fabrics for the individual design elements. However, some design pieces lend themselves to different materials, and many fun fabrics exist. Don't forget to look in your closets for possibilities or consider some of the following novelty fabrics.

Calico—Small prints for visual interest.

Terry cloth—Great for sheep or for banners that children can touch.

Plush felt—Fun texture for kids.

Also consider *metallic fabrics, taffeta, satin, Liquid Gold, organdy,* or *nonwoven interfacing* (with the fibers showing). Any of these, plus numerous other fabric types, can be selected, but make sure the fabric for the design piece will adhere in an attractive way to the background fabric.

The sale table in the fabric store offers a source for inexpensive specialty touches for your banners.

Additional materials for design elements

A trip to a knitting shop or craft store will delight your creative senses just as much as one to a fabric store. Yarn, ribbon, paint, and more can enhance the banner's design when you embroider, glue, or paint on the surface.

Here's a short list of materials that can help you add those finishing touches.

- Yarn, embroidery floss, or metallic thread
- Ribbon
- Rickrack
- Corded piping, middy braid, soutache trim
- Seam binding
- Bias tape—available in single-fold or double-fold
- Buttons, coins, old jewelry—garage sales and flea markets offer endless possibilities
- Beads—bead shops, too, will spur your imagination and offer visual delights

BONDING FABRICS AND MATERIALS

- Double-stick tape
- Masking tape
- Sobo brand glue by Delta or Aleene's brand tacky glue (white craft glues suitable for use with most fabrics)
- Pellon Wonder-Under, Aleene's Ultra Hold Fusible Web, and Therm O Web HeatnBond brands iron-on adhesive come in different weights and several colors
- Stitch-Witchery brand iron-on bonding web
- Basting fabric adhesive
- Pressing cloth—a piece of 100 percent cotton muslin, a cotton tea towel, or a cotton bedsheet

OUTLINING MATERIALS

Opaque paint markers, fabric markers, fabric paint pens, acrylic squeeze paints, and puff paints provide options for outlining individual design elements.

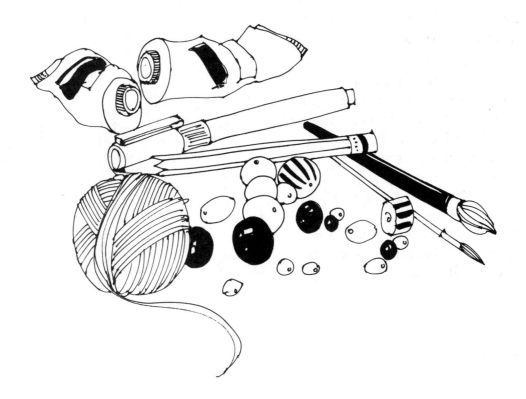

SELECTING COLORS

Color suggestions accompany most of the banner designs, but they are only suggestions. A good way to experiment with color is to make several photocopies of the design, purchase a set of brush markers (made by Marvy, Staedtler, or Tombo) at an art supply store, and try different color schemes on the photocopies. Brush markers allow you to fill in large areas quickly and evenly so you will have an idea of the finished look.

For artists and designers the study of color is lifelong, but a brief look at color theory might be helpful for bannermakers. For starters, think about how God combines colors in nature—in sunsets; in marine life; in rich, lush foliage; in arid desert climates; in winter (think of all the different whites); in evening (what colors are shadows?). Immediately you sense unlimited possibilities, but you also are aware that some color combinations don't work or irritate the eye. Refer to the color wheel on page 91 and consider a few of these reliable basic color schemes that *do* work.

1. **Monochromatic**—a series of different shades or tints of *one* hue. Sky blue, navy, cornflower blue, and midnight blue, for example, would create a monochromatic color scheme. Because all the colors belong to the same family, this combination usually creates a peaceful, integrated feeling.

2. **Analogous**—a combination of colors that appear next to each other on the color wheel. Combining red, orange, and yellow, for example, forms a scheme that works because the colors are all very much *like* one another. This also translates into a feeling of wholeness and harmony.

3. **Complementary**—colors that are opposite each other on the color wheel. Sometimes a design requires colors that offer excitement rather than peacefulness. That's the feeling a complementary color scheme produces. Red and green, for example, are as far away from each other on the color wheel as possible and are, therefore, as unalike as possible. They create a stimulating, sometimes even jarring, effect. With a complementary color scheme, one color usually predominates and the other is added for punch.

4. **Triadic**—three colors that are equidistant on the color wheel. For example, the primary colors—red, blue, and yellow—form a triad and create a bouncy, exciting look. Triadic colors probably afford the most fun and, therefore, produce a more lighthearted, whimsical look. But they also can create a feeling of strength, just like three points determine a plane in geometry.

Color temperature also has an effect on the perceived message of the banner. Warm colors—colors that have yellow in them like gold, orange, Chinese red, yellow-green, etc.—move forward, enveloping the viewer and drawing the viewer into the scene. Cool colors that contain blue—purple, violet, turquoise, cool greens, etc.—recede from the eye and create a more serious tone.

Church tradition is another prominent consideration for color. The following colors are accompanied by their symbolic meanings in the worship environment.

- **White**—a festival color in the church; appropriate for Christmas, Easter, the transfiguration, Epiphany, Trinity, All Saints' Day; symbolizes purity, truth, innocence, holiness, redemption; if used as a background color, it can overwhelm design elements unless they are bold in shape and design

- **Blue**—appropriate for Advent (optional); symbolizes hope, heaven, truth, beginnings

- **Red**—appropriate for the Day of Pentecost, Reformation, Palm Sunday, Maundy Thursday; symbolizes love, fire, the Holy Spirit, royalty, sin, sacrifice

- **Gold**—appropriate for Easter; symbolizes royalty, blessings

- **Green**—appropriate for the Pentecost and Epiphany seasons; symbolizes growth, fruitfulness, abundance

- **Violet**—appropriate for Lent, Advent (optional), Palm Sunday; symbolizes repentance, royalty, solemnity, sorrow, grief

- **Black**—appropriate for Ash Wednesday and Good Friday; symbolizes sin, death, sorrow, absence; if used as a background color, design elements will appear to advance from the background

Although color plays an important part in conveying the message of the text and design, don't be overwhelmed by the prospect of choosing. Your instincts and your awareness of the many ways color is used in the church and in the world will serve you well.

BASIC MATERIALS FOR ASSEMBLY

- Scissors—one pair for paper and one for fabric
- Butcher paper, craft, or pattern paper by the roll
- Nonwoven tracing fabric—inexpensive alternative to paper for making pattern pieces
- Masking tape
- Clear 12″ ruler, yardstick, and tape measure
- Colored pencils—light and dark colors
- Disappearing fabric marker—for drawing guidelines on background fabrics
- T-square
- Compass

ENLARGING PATTERNS

The designs in this book easily can be converted from inches to feet. For example, the tall, rectangular shape of many of the these banners would change from the pictured 4″ × 8½″ to a 4′ × 8½′ finished banner. However, by using an opaque projector or overhead projector, the finished banner becomes whatever size you wish.

The first step is to photocopy the selected banner design so you won't have to fit a bulky book into the projector. Then follow one of these three options for enlarging the pattern.

1. **Opaque Projector**—This is by far the easiest method for enlarging a banner design to create the pattern pieces. You probably will have access to an opaque projector through your church or school. After taping butcher paper (the rolled butcher paper that your church uses for disposable table-cloths is ideal) or craft paper to a wall, place the photocopy in the opaque projector. Then move the projector toward or away from the wall until the projected image is the desired size. (It's easiest to use a tape measure to size the banner as it's projected on the wall.) Using a pencil, trace the design onto the butcher paper. Before taking the pattern down, turn off the projector and carefully check the pattern for any untraced elements. Remove this pattern and tape another sheet of butcher paper to the wall. Without moving the projector, trace the design again on this sheet of butcher paper so you have duplicate designs on two large pieces of paper.

2. **Overhead Transparency Projector**—This also is an easy method, but it requires a sheet of acetate transparency film, available at most copy shops. After making a photocopy of the banner design from the book, make a copy of the "copy" on the transparency film by hand feeding the film into the photocopier. Use this transparent film on an overhead transparency projector. Then, follow the steps described for the opaque projector to size and trace the design.

3. If neither of the projector machines is available, the age-old **grid method** of enlarging will do the job. After making a photocopy of the banner design, carefully draw a 1″-square grid on the photocopy. On butcher paper, use a tape measure and T-square to mark the outer dimensions of the enlarged banner (for example, 4′ × 8½′). Keeping the proportions the same,

carefully draw square grid lines on your banner pattern. (In our example, the enlarged banner would have a 1′-square grid.) Using a pencil (and keeping an eraser handy), draw the design on the butcher paper using the grids to eyeball the lines. (See diagram on this page for an example of this method.) This method takes time and is not as accurate as the other two, but you will feel more ownership in the finished product because you've sketched it yourself and perhaps made a few improvements in the process. (It's the opportunity to do your own thing!)

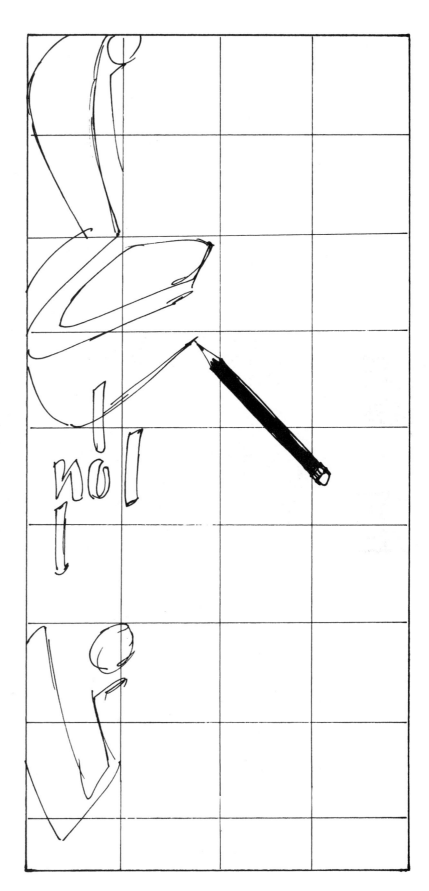

CUTTING THE BACKGROUND

If the background fabric is washable, wash it, dry it, cut off the selvage edges, and iron it. If the background fabric is not washable, drape it over a horizontally held pole to see how it hangs. If it hangs nicely, you probably can use the finished selvage edges as they are and eliminate any finishing of the side edges.

With the fabric prepared, place it face down on a large flat surface in a well-lit area. The floor, your kitchen breakfast counter, or one of those large tables in your church's fellowship hall or Sunday school rooms will work. Carefully cut out one of the paper patterns you've made (so the outside edges of the paper pattern are the same as the outside dimensions of the finished banner). Place the pattern on top of the outstretched fabric. Pin it in place. Use a disappearing fabric marker to draw a line ½″ from either side, 1½″ from the bottom, and 3″ from the top. Cut the background fabric following these lines. You may need to apply an anti-fraying agent, such as Dritz Fray Check, to the cut edges.

French seams offer another possibility for constructing the background of banners 4, 23, 24, 25, 26, 29, 43, 46, 48, and 58. French seams allow part of the design to be seen from the back of the banner, which is advantageous for processional banners or for ones that hang from the rafters of the church. Using French seams for the background allows you to use several different colors for the base or background of the banner and also makes the assembly of curved edges easy. French seams provide fuller possibilities by creating a beautiful, finished look on both sides of the banner. Thus, viewers from both directions can enjoy the various background colors. The diagram on page 20 describes the use of French seams for Banner 26.

CUTTING THE BACKGROUND

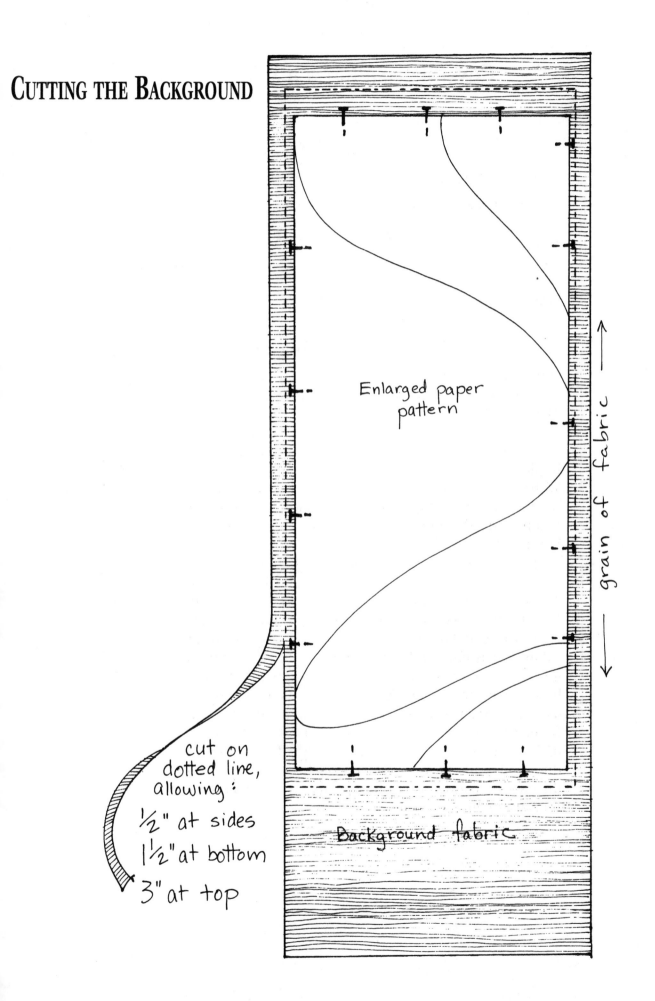

Enlarged paper pattern

grain of fabric

cut on dotted line, allowing:

½" at sides

1½" at bottom

3" at top

Background fabric

CONSTRUCTING FRENCH SEAMS

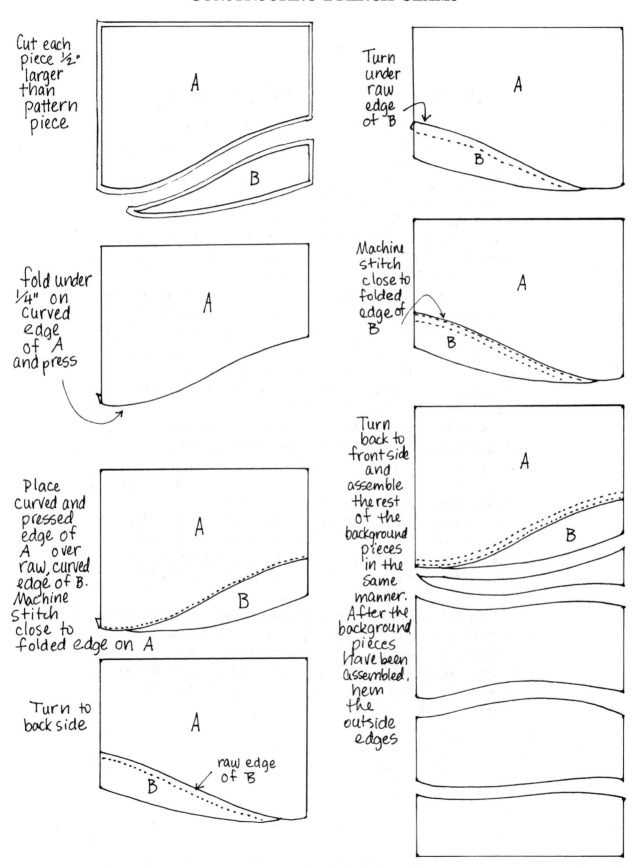

Cut each piece ½" larger than pattern piece

A

B

Turn under raw edge of B

A

B

fold under ¼" on curved edge of A and press

A

Machine stitch close to folded edge of B

A

B

Place curved and pressed edge of A over raw, curved edge of B. Machine stitch close to folded edge on A

A

B

Turn back to front side and assemble the rest of the background pieces in the same manner. After the background pieces have been assembled, hem the outside edges

A

B

Turn to back side

A

raw edge of B

B

CUTTING OUT THE DESIGN ELEMENTS

You have traced two patterns for a good reason—to help you keep track of where all those individual pieces go once you've cut them out. (One pattern remains whole; the other will be cut in pieces.) Before you cut out the individual elements, number each piece and mark a *T* at the top. Then transfer the numbers to the intact pattern or your photocopy from the book. Then, cut all the separate pieces from the paper pattern. Place each piece on top of its matching shape on the uncut paper pattern.

As with the background fabric, wash, dry, and iron any washable fabrics to be used for design elements. Lay the fabric on a flat surface. Pin a few design elements at a time to their respective fabrics and cut them out. If the shapes will be flush with other shapes in the finished design, add a ¼″ edge so the adjacent shapes can overlap. This creates a smoother surface.

After you cut out each piece, place it on top of its matching shape on the uncut paper pattern to keep things organized and to prevent long sighs and future grumpiness. If you have a spot (a room, a counter, a Ping-Pong table in the garage) that you can make off-limits to outside traffic for the duration of the banner's assembly, you are indeed blessed. But that is a luxury, and banner-makers usually are required to be flexible, make-do people who come up with an organizing system that works for them.

An alternative to making two paper patterns and cutting one apart for the pattern pieces is to make one paper pattern and trace the individual pieces onto inexpensive sheer (see-through) fabric. The fabric is easier to work with than paper because it doesn't slide around, tear, or bunch.

LETTERING

The letters that appear on many of these banner designs are from calligraphic alphabets that feature thick and thin lines. These lines are achieved by the calligrapher's pen and brush strokes. The contrast between these thick and thin lines gives the letters their beauty and offers artistic possibilities to bannermakers. The alphabets on pages 23–24 are only two of countless calligraphy styles. Each one produces a unique look. They are included to aid your future banner designs, as well as offer you options for the construction of the banners in this book. The alphabets provided can be enlarged on a photocopier or by using one of the methods described in the section "Enlarging Patterns" (page 16–17). Additional alphabet ideas can be found in typography or calligraphy books at the library. Or you can use a computer-generated alphabet or create your own.

Italic letters produce an exquisite, rather formal appearance, which works well with Scripture verses. Some capital letters in these alphabets have flourishes and are meant to be combined only with small letters, not with one another. (Words that use all capital letters require a simpler, unadorned style.)

The *brush* lettering alphabet has a more casual, flowing appearance. It offers many possibilities to bannermakers. It's versatile, too, because it can communicate strength or directness. If arranged freely, it can give a lighthearted, joyful look to your design to complement a joyous Gospel message.

Letters look best if they are allowed to fit together naturally rather than in methodically measured spaces. When it's time to apply the lettering, draw only a few base lines for the letters and eyeball the spacing. You will have more fun allowing the letters to find their own places, nestling close to one another.

Italic Typeface

a b c d e f g h i j k

l m n o p q r s t u

v w x y and z

A B C D E F G

H I J K L M N

O P Q R S T U

V W X Y and Z

Brush Typeface

a b c d e f g h i j
k l m n o p q r s
t u v w x y z

A B C D E F G
H I J K L M N
O P Q R S T U V
W X Y and Z

Adhering the Design Elements to the Background

Another reminder that you are not only the banner assembler but the artist: When arranging the shapes and letters of the design on the background, you have much latitude. Referring to the paper pattern is helpful, but seeing other possibilities and using your sense of design is fun too.

1. **Gluing Method**—Gluing the pieces of the banner together is an easy and usually acceptable method of assembly. Sobo brand glue by Delta or Aleene's brand tacky glue works well with many fabrics, but it is best to experiment by gluing a few scraps of the design fabrics to a scrap of the background fabric. How does it look? Imagine the entire banner done this way. If it looks good, glue probably will be fine.

   Start placing a few design pieces on the banner background, referring to the intact paper pattern to see where things go. However, feel free to let the pieces arrange themselves because you may see other possibilities in the composition as you go along. You will recognize the order in which things must be glued, depending on the individual banner.

As a general rule, if two elements overlap, glue the bottom piece first. As you glue each piece, use a T-square or ruler to keep one side of the piece in place as you lift up the other side, apply the glue, and place it back down on the background. When that is dry, do the same to the other half of the piece.

2. **Iron-on Adhesive Method**—Pellon Wonder-Under, Aleene's Ultra Hold Fusible Web, Therm O Web HeatnBond, and Stitch Witchery are bonding fabrics that make banner assembly easier and give the shapes a more integrated look. Use a disappearing fabric marker to provide reference lines on the banner background fabric to ensure that the shapes are bonded in the right places. (Be sure to try the marker on scrap fabric first.) Again, let your design ideas come into play. Create a composition that works for you. The pattern is only a suggestion!

All iron-on adhesives come with complete directions and helpful suggestions. Pellon Wonder-Under is probably an easier process for adhering individual design pieces. Stitch Witchery is better for pieces that have long, straight edges. Experiment with all the fusible web products on a variety of fabrics to see which combinations work best.

3. **Machine Stitching Method**—This method is time consuming, but it produces a beautiful banner. It will work best if you back each design piece with fusible interfacing to prevent the edges from fraying. (Or use an anti-fraying agent such as Dritz Fray Check.) Place several design pieces in their spots on the background fabric, referring to the paper pattern. You might want to make some reference lines with a disappearing fabric marker. Remember, you have the freedom to place the design elements in your own arrangement. Pin or baste the pieces in place and use a zig-zag or straight stitch on your sewing machine to attach the pieces.

4. **Running Stitch Method**—A few banners were designed to achieve a just-barely-attached look that would create a feeling of lightness and movement. Banners 9, 14, 22, 37, 47, and 52 can be assembled in a variety of ways, but using a hand-sewn running stitch would be a fast, attractive way to interpret the design. No need to back the design pieces with interfacing; if the edges unravel a little, so much the better. The patterns and directions for these banners indicate how this method is to be implemented. The lettering on these banners, however, could be attached with glue or an iron-on adhesive so it appears more stable.

FINISHING TOUCHES

Ideas for special design touches accompany each banner. Your thoughts as you work also will provide novel ideas that will make your banner a one-of-a-kind work of art.

Hand-cut rubber stamps made from erasers and fabric ink pads provide a fast method for applying a repetitive design element (a leaf or a star, for example). The more elaborate process of block printing (directions accompany Banner 45) also creates a unique look.

Gluing or stitching found objects onto the banner gives a surprise feature to the design. A variety of bells and pieces of jewelry enhance the blissful message of Banner 8, craft sticks could be the perfect fence for Banner 10, and specialty yarn or cord found in a weaving shop would lend a happy note to Banner 12. Large purple or green buttons make great grapes for Banner 17, and the scraps of trim in the shoe box in your hall closet could find a permanent home on Banner 18. The directions for Banner 39 ask you to use colorful ticket stubs, campaign buttons, or commemorative stamps to communicate a personal celebration. These items, or others, can be souvenirs that illustrate the fullness God lavishes upon you in countless ways.

Some designs can be enhanced by outlining. This can be done in a variety of ways. Several items are available at craft stores, and each creates a unique look. Opaque paint markers, fabric markers, fabric paint pens, acrylic squeeze paints, and puff paints come in many beautiful colors, but you'll need to experiment with them on individual fabrics. The squeeze paints require a little practice and give a more informal appearance to your banner. If you are an experienced painter, acrylic paints or even watercolors can be applied with brushes wherever you feel the design could be enriched. Yarn can effectively outline shapes but requires some care when gluing.

Perhaps the consummate touch of elegance, if time permits, is embroidery. Several banners in this collection lend themselves to some sort of stitchery. Embroidery floss, metallic thread, or yarn can create a beautiful, artistic finale to your project. Suggestions for stitchery appear with several banners, but your creative energy also will supply ideas for embroidery. Any open area in a design provides an opportunity for the flowing lines that decorative stitchery offers. A review of a few basic stitches appears to the right.

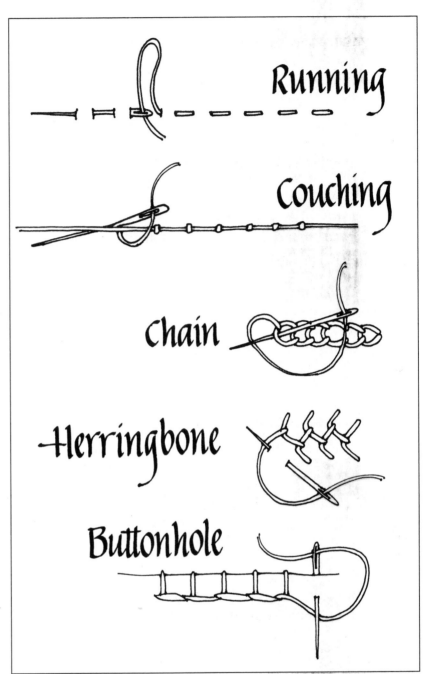

COMPLETING THE BANNER

1. **Unlined Method**—If the background fabric is sturdy enough, your banner probably can be hemmed with a straight machine stitch. Use a ½″ hem on the sides, a 1½″ hem on the bottom. To make the hanging casement, lay the banner face down. Mark a line 6″ from the top. Fold the top down to the line and stitch in place. Instead of machine stitching, the bottom and side hems can be bonded with strips of iron-on adhesive. The top hem, however, which must bear the weight of the banner, should be machine stitched.

2. **Line with fusible interfacing**— Place the banner face down on your work surface and cut the fusible interfacing the same size as the banner background. Be sure to read the instructions that come with the interfacing before you bond the fabrics using an iron and a damp pressing cloth. (Experimenting first with a small piece of the background fabric and the interfac-

ing is always wise.) To make the hanging casement, lay the banner face down. Mark a line 6″ from the top. Fold the top down to the line and stitch in place. Because perfectly matching the edges of the banner background and the interfacing is impossible, neatly trim the edges after applying the interfacing.

3. **Line with a lightweight fabric—** Use the bonding method. First, cut the lining fabric to match the size of the banner background. Then, lay the banner face down, place strips of Stitch Witchery brand iron-on bonding web along the edges, and carefully position the lining on top. Use a damp pressing cloth and an iron to press the three layers together. (Be sure to read the directions that come with Stitch Witchery.) To make

the hanging casement, lay the banner face down. Mark a line 6″ from the top. Fold the top down to the line and stitch in place.

4. **Sewing method—**This method is probably the best one for the banner designs in this book that have chevron, angled, or circular bottom edges. Cut the lining fabric to match the size of the background banner fabric. With right sides together, machine stitch along the side and bottom edges. After trimming the corners and clipping any curves, turn right side out and press the seams. Baste the top edge together. To make the hanging casement, lay the banner face down. Mark a line 6″ from the top. Fold the top down to the line and stitch in place.

Now you are finished. I hope the creation of your banner was an act of worship for you and, if you were working with others, an opportunity for Christian fellowship. Solving the problems involved with a bulky project like this; making the decisions on colors, materials, and design; seeing how the Holy Spirit uses your creativity and gives you the stick-to-itiveness to stay with such a big project; running out to the fabric store just one more time to pick up the item that will provide the final, perfect touch all add up to an enormous task. May your worshiping community find in this banner a source of beauty, joy, comfort, and inspiration. And may your prayer upon completion echo other artists who dedicate their work to our Creator: "Lord, bless my work to Your glory and our good."

OLD TESTAMENT BANNERS

Banner 1—Genesis 1:26

Then God said, "Let Us make man in Our image, in Our likeness, and let them rule over the fish of the sea and the birds of the air, over the livestock, over all the earth, and over all the creatures that move along the ground." Genesis 1:26

What fun God had in His good work of creation. The design echoes the variety of His work. The whimsical folk art style suggests using bright primary colors and surrounding all the shapes with an embroidered buttonhole stitch or herringbone stitch in a contrasting color. Rickrack could provide the lines on the crocodile and fish. The sturdy lettering style is a reminder of the solemn responsibility God entrusted to us when He gave us His gifts in nature. The panel behind the Scripture verse could be a separate background piece in a contrasting color.

Banner 2—
Numbers
6:26

The LORD bless you and keep you; the LORD make His face shine upon you and be gracious to you; the LORD turn His face toward you and give you peace.
Numbers 6:24–26

The traditional end-of-service Aaronic blessing proclaims our confidence in the Lord and sends us forth in joy. In the pastor's words, the Lord Himself is smiling upon us, giving us His Spirit and His strength for the days to come. The abstract shapes bouncing around the letters could incorporate a variety of bright colors, each one a different combination of colors—turquoise, dark yellow, red, violet, spring green.

Banner 3— Deuteronomy 33:27

The eternal God is your refuge, and underneath are the everlasting arms. He will drive out your enemy before you. Deuteronomy 33:27

Moses' final words to the Israelites remind us that our God is our victorious protector. The colors should be royal— purple, gold, and white. Security is what the Scripture passage offers, and the solid symmetry of the design reinforces that.

The top portion of the cruciform shape is a castle turret that also suggests a crown. The robe and arms form the remainder of the cross shape, symbolizing God's arms that bear us up, that flow with blessings, and that went to the cross for us. The design pieces that become streamers could be done with wide grosgrain ribbon sewn on with mitered corners.

THE ETERNAL GOD IS YOUR REFUGE· UNDERNEATH ARE THE EVERLASTING ARMS

Mitered corner

33

Banner 4–
Joshua 24:15

And if you be unwilling to serve the LORD, choose this day whom you will serve, whether the gods your fathers served in the region beyond the River, or the gods of the Amorites in whose land you dwell; but as for me and my house, we will serve the LORD. Joshua 24:15 RSV

Joshua's joyful pledge is one that we are to live out in our neighborhoods and in our daily activities. The large curved background shapes depict the possibly enormous results of those sometimes small actions. Those shapes may be adhered to a single background piece, or for a more dramatic effect, they could be assembled using French seams (see page 20) to form the background themselves.

Banner 5—
2 Samuel
22:3

[David] said: "The LORD is my rock, my fortress and my deliverer; my God is my rock, in whom I take refuge, my shield and the horn of my salvation. He is my stronghold, my refuge and my savior—from violent men You save me. 2 Samuel 22:2–3

After the Lord delivered David from his ene-mies, including King Saul, David was inspired to sing the words of our text. The words are inter-spersed with building block shapes to form a strong, fortress-like structure. The design calls for strong colors too—red, black, gold.

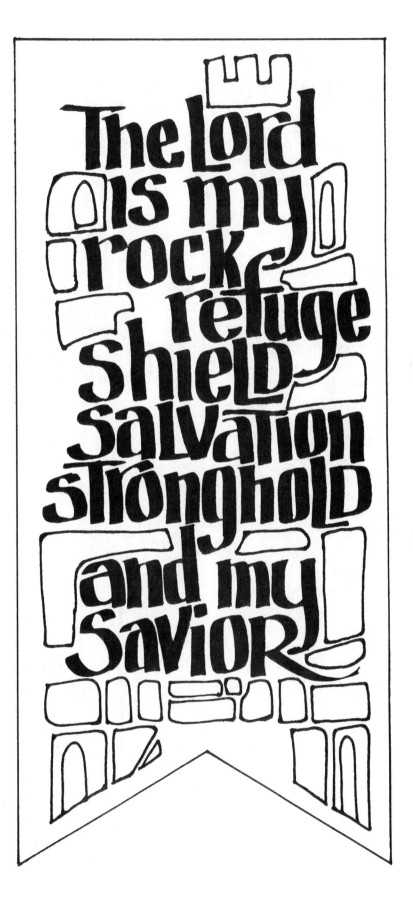

Banner 6—
Psalm 23:6

Surely goodness and mercy shall follow me all the days of my life, and I shall dwell in the house of the LORD my whole life long. Psalm 23:6 NRSV

The parallel banners call for bright blue backgrounds with contrasting bright yellow grains and sun. Black buttons could provide the dots that decorate each panel. And bright yellow craft yarn in an embroidered chain stitch (see page 27) could form the heads of grain. Use a black paint marker to outline the sun and to draw the grain stalks.

Detail of grain

Banner 7– Psalm 27:1

The LORD is my light and my salvation—whom shall I fear? The LORD is the stronghold of my life—of whom shall I be afraid? Psalm 27:1

We trust that the sun will rise every day and that its light will bring joy to our lives. How much more joy it brings us to know and trust the God who created the sun and ordered it to shine. He is our light and has revealed to us His Son, Jesus, our Savior. The sun bursting forth would be stunning with gold star studs dotting the circles. (Easy-to-follow directions for attaching the studs are found on the package.)

Banner 8—
Psalm 30:5

For His anger is but for a moment, His favor is for life; weeping may endure for a night, but joy comes in the morning. Psalm 30:5 NKJV

There is no reason a banner can't be auditory. And why not a banner with windows too? The interior spaces of the *O*s provide natural places for openings and for the addition of bells. If the banner is used in a procession, the ringing bells can reinforce the joyful message of the psalm. Use ⅛″ ribbon to attach any type of lightweight bell. And who says the bells have to match? (A variety of sizes and types would create a variety of sounds.) To make the windows, cut out the fabric inside the *O*s. Use a machine stitch to sew on double-fold bias tape around the raw edge. Attach the bells.

Overlap double-fold bias tape on circular opening. Machine stitch close to folded edge.

Banner 9 — Psalm 37:5

Commit your way to the LORD; trust in Him, and He will act.
Psalm 37:5 NRSV

This church community banner signifies our joint commitment to the Lord and our individual ones too. Because it proclaims that God has acted for us through Jesus' death and resurrection, as well as through personal and daily actions on our behalf, the banner would be appropriate for a church building project, a stewardship campaign, spiritual renewal, or a church anniversary.

First, ask each member to bring in a fabric scrap that expresses his or her personality. Cut each scrap into a cross shape. (Don't use a pattern; the variety of cross shapes will make the banner even better.) Arrange the crosses to form one giant cross. There's no need to finish the edges of the crosses either; instead, use a running stitch to attach them to the background (see diagram). Allow the edges of the individual crosses to move if a summer breeze comes through.

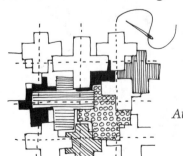

Attaching the crosses

COMMIT YOUR WAY TO THE LORD

TRUST IN HIM AND HE WILL ACT

Banners 10 and 11— Psalm 46:10; Psalm 121:2

Be still, and know that I am God; I will be exalted among the nations, I will be exalted in the earth. Psalm 46:10

My help comes from the LORD, the Maker of heaven and earth. Psalm 121:2

These companion banners bear witness to God's steadfastness and should be displayed together. Consider using color (yellows and oranges) on the two suns and using only black for the letters and landscape. Arrange the design elements on an off-white background for a dramatic effect.

Banner 12 –
Psalm 51:10

Create in me a clean heart,
O God, and put a new and
right spirit within me.
Psalm 51:10 NRSV

The heart in this design is askew, just like human hearts, but beauty can proceed from it (represented by the colorful ribbon streamers) when God cleanses and forgives and does His good work through us. The ribbons should hang loosely from the heart and extend below the bottom hem. This banner would be an attractive addition to an outdoor service with the breeze moving the streamers.

Banner 13—Psalm 66:5

Come and see what God has done, how awesome His works in man's behalf! Psalm 66:5

Come and see? How can we miss it? This design celebrates God's sparkling creation and His showers of blessings, all in swirling activity. The swirl shapes and the sun can be cut from gold metallic fabric. Contrasting black triangles can fill in the negative spaces between the elements. Use a pencil eraser dipped in gold metallic acrylic paint to randomly stamp the dots on the background fabric. Black letters and an off-white background complete the banner.

Swirl shape

Banner 14 – Psalm 91:11

For He will command His angels concerning you to guard you in all your ways. Psalm 91:11

Use semi-transparent fabrics for this banner. Heavyweight interfacing is a good background fabric, and inexpensive starched organdy makes excellent angel wings and sleeves. Rather than gluing or fusing the wings and sleeves to the background, use gold metallic thread to do a running stitch across the top of each wing piece and around the sleeve pieces, as indicated by the dashed lines in the design (bottom layers first). Allow the wing pieces to extend beyond the edge of the banner. Use gold metallic fabric for the circle shapes behind the angel; tan fabric for face and hands; and white fabric for hair. Use black for the letters and a black paint marker for the lines on the hands, face, and hair. Hanging the banner away from the wall creates one kind of semi-transparent effect; hanging it flush with a dark colored wall creates another.

HE WILL COMMAND HIS ANGELS TO GUARD YOU IN ALL YOUR WAYS

Banner 15—Psalm 103:8

The LORD is compassionate and gracious, slow to anger, abounding in love.
Psalm 103:8

Use a gradation of blues and greens and comforting, flowing lines to interpret this peaceful promise in a banner trio. The long flourishes on the letters symbolize God's hand reaching into our lives. The gentle s-curves communicate a message of solace. To achieve a three-dimensional appearance, put a layer of ⅛″ quilt batting between the design pieces and the background fabric. A chain stitch (see page 27) could further delineate the colors. Another possibility is to use French seams (see page 20) and allow the design pieces to form the background.

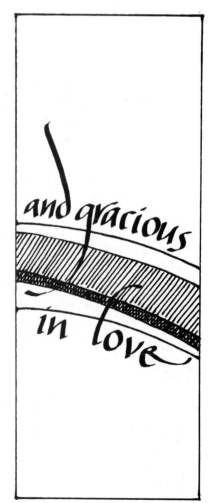

Banner 16—Psalm 103:22

Praise the LORD, all His works everywhere in His dominion.
Praise the LORD, O my soul. Psalm 103:22

This banner could be assembled quickly by gluing the simple flower and leaf shapes to a solid background. Or it could be enhanced with decorative stitching around and through the flowers and leaves. Use ribbon to border the letters, and allow it to trail into streamers off the edge of the banner.

Banner 17 — Psalm 104:28

When You give to them, they gather it up; when You open Your hand, they are filled with good things. Psalm 104:28 NRSV

Both our daily physical needs that God meets with daily bread and our spiritual needs that are met with the Sacrament are represented here in the good things that God provides. The fish could be done in layers of a gradation of blues or greens. The wheat could be embroidered with heavy yarn using a chain embroidery stitch (see page 27).

46

This is the day the LORD has made; let us rejoice and be glad in it.
Psalm 118:24

This is the place to use those colorful calicos, polka-dots, and striped fabrics in your scrap bag to create a vibrant landscape that celebrates the Lord's mercies to us each day. The center panel could take on a three-dimensional look by placing ⅛″ quilt batting between the fabric for the sun and hills and the background fabric. Either use a machine zig-zag stitch to secure the edges of the separate pieces or use a straight machine stitch on top of bias tape (in a complementary color) that overlaps the abutting edges. The bias tape adds a bright outline to the fields and hides the raw edges. You could even take the sewing a step further with the addition of quilting throughout the landscape pieces.

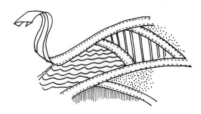

Outlining with bias tape

Banner 19 — Psalm 119:105

Your word is a lamp to my feet and a light for my path. Psalm 119:105

The bold letters parallel the psalmist's bold claim. A black embroidered chain stitch (see page 27) fills the counter spaces of the black letters. The same effect could be achieved with a black paint marker. The flames will create glowing spots of color (use a gradation of yellows and oranges) on the black-and-white panels.

Banner 20—Ecclesiastes 3:1

To everything there is a season, a time for every purpose under heaven.
Ecclesiastes 3:1 NKJV

God-created life cycles are illustrated on this banner. Because the design is a traditional treatment of these well-loved words, why not use an unconventional color scheme? Consider shades of purple, blue, and lavender for the entire design instead of the familiar winter, spring, summer, and autumn colors.

For to us a child is born, to us a son is given, and the government will be on His shoulders. And He will be called Wonderful Counselor, Mighty God, Everlasting Father, Prince of Peace. Isaiah 9:6

A deep blue background recalls the Bethlehem night sky and offers high contrast to the angels, gleaming in white with metallic gold fabric wings and trumpets. The words in Roman capitals need gold as well to accompany Isaiah's royal message. Embroidery, decorative trim, or ribbon could be added to the angels' gowns to create a regal banner.

Banner 22—
Isaiah 40:31

Those who hope in the LORD will renew their strength. They will soar on wings like eagles; they will run and not grow weary, they will walk and not be faint. Isaiah 40:31

Consider a vibrant red background instead of a traditional blue sky to signify the excitement that God has in store for us. Using inexpensive starched organdy for the eagle's separate wing pieces creates an interesting see-through effect. Attaching them (bottom layers first) with gold thread in a running stitch along the top of each piece, as indicated by the dashed lines in the design, allows the ends to move. And movement is what the passage is all about.

THEY WILL SOAR

ON WINGS LIKE EAGLES THEY WILL RUN AND NOT GROW WEARY

Banner 23— Isaiah 40:31

Those who hope in the LORD will renew their strength. They will soar on wings like eagles; they will run and not grow weary, they will walk and not be faint. Isaiah 40:31

This passage in Isaiah offers too many graphic ideas for only one treatment. This time the direction is up also, indicating the uphill path Christians sometimes climb. But as we climb, the Lord always provides the strength we need to continue. You could use French seams (see page 20) to make the banner background. Use shades of red, purple, gold, and white for the s-curve of the path.

Banner 24—Isaiah 43:1

But now thus says the LORD, *He who created you, O Jacob, He who formed you, O Israel: Do not fear, for I have redeemed you; I have called you by name, you are Mine. Isaiah 43:1 NRSV*

Two contrasting colors form the four squares of the background, which in turn creates a cross. The decisive brush strokes of the lettering reiterate God's strong call to us in Baptism. The symbols of baptism (the water and shell) can be sewn or bonded. Use either contrasting printed fabrics or various solid colors to make the "layers" of water. If you use solid colors, consider adding "wave" lines with embroidery or paint markers. An alternative is a three-dimensional treatment accomplished by adding quilt batting behind the shell and waves. Quilt the fine lines for a dramatic effect.

See, I am doing a new thing! Now it springs up; do you not perceive it?
I am making a way in the desert and streams in the wasteland.
Isaiah 43:19

This design is a reminder of the new life that God can bring from a desert or from a dried-up life. Semi-transparent fabric in shades of blue, green, and turquoise could provide the water shape. The fabric could be cut free-form and sewn on with the pieces overlapping one another. A bold blue running stitch of embroidery floss could provide the outlines. Beads could be added for pebbles.

Banner 26 — Isaiah 46:4

Even to your old age and gray hairs I am He, I am He who will sustain you. I have made you and I will carry you; I will sustain you and I will rescue you. Isaiah 46:4

Notice that God's promise is in the bedrock *under* the wind, waves, and tempests. Stark gray, black, and white forms, combined with red lettering, would proclaim the message powerfully. The fine lines in the waves can be ignored or applied with a paint marker. Because the background shapes are fairly simple, the banner base could be sewn with French seams (see page 20) from panels of varying gray fabrics. Richly textured upholstery fabrics might be a good choice for this background.

Banner 27—Isaiah 55:12

You will go out in joy and be led forth in peace; the mountains and hills will burst into song before you, and all the trees of the field will clap their hands. Isaiah 55:12

The free-form shapes complement the joyful news of Isaiah's words. Ribbons and fabric in bright colors also can enhance the message. Shapes and ribbons can veer off in all directions if they are attached only at the top and allowed to hang freely.

Banner 28 – Isaiah 61:1

The Spirit of the Lord GOD is upon me, because the LORD has anointed me; He has sent me to bring good news to the oppressed, to bind up the broken-hearted, to proclaim liberty to the captives, and release to the prisoners. Isaiah 61:1 NRSV

The heart motif never gets old, perhaps because that's where God's work is done. This easily constructed banner can use fabric from the scrap bag. A buttonhole stitch (see page 27) around the patch, and perhaps the heart too, will add a special touch.

Banner 29—
Jeremiah
31:3

The Lord appeared to us in the past, saying: "I have loved you with an everlasting love; I have drawn you with loving-kindness." Jeremiah 31:3

The flowing lines through the word "everlasting" symbolize the way God's love flows through our lives. The background of this banner could be constructed from three separate pieces so the center panel could be worked on separately. The striped area represents two pieces of fabric that run horizontally across the middle section of the banner. The letters for "everlasting," cut from contrasting fabrics, are placed on top of the horizontal strips of fabric.

NEW TESTAMENT BANNERS

Banner 30—Matthew 1:21

She will give birth to a son, and you are to give Him the name Jesus, because He will save His people from their sins. Matthew 1:21

The medallion shape of the virgin and child brings to mind a theme of circles, wholeness, completeness, "in the fullness of time." Use an embroidered back stitch or couching stitch (see page 27) or a paint marker for the facial features and the lines in the hair and swaddling clothes. Mary's dress can be several shades of blue and turquoise. Decorative trim or additional embroidery can enhance her head covering. Add rosy cheeks to mother and baby with a crayon or use makeup blush.

61

Banner 31 —
Matthew 5:8

*Blessed are the pure in heart,
for they shall see God.
Matthew 5:8 RSV*

This is the time to pull out all the stops and cut and paste to your heart's desire. Of course, the shapes for "Pure in Heart" are there for tracing, but you'll have more fun if you assemble scraps of your favorite colors, cut them into pieces of approximately the same height, back them with iron-on adhesive, and cut letter shapes free-form. You'll do better than you think (especially if you recall the fun of those long-ago kindergarten days). You'll also have the satisfaction of being your own designer. Rickrack, buttons, sequins, and stitchery can enhance the original shapes and add to the celebration that awaits the "pure in heart"!

Banner 32—Matthew 5:16

In the same way, let your light shine before men, that they may see your good deeds and praise your Father in heaven. Matthew 5:16

The positive/negative treatment of the candle flames indicates the way we are to complement one another as we work in God's kingdom. Leading, following, sharing the light, taking turns, holding up the light for someone else—all this allows God-given personalities and talents to shine. Yellow, gold, and red can provide a checkerboard pattern for the flames on this three-panel banner.

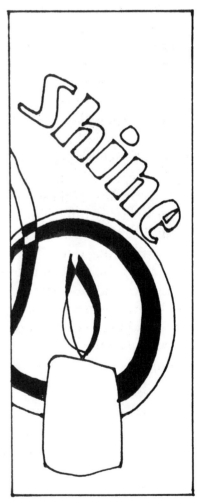

Banner 33—
Matthew 6:28

And why do you worry about clothing? Consider the lilies of the field, how they grow; they neither toil nor spin. Matthew 6:28 NRSV

Our Lord's gentle admonition reminds us of our complete dependence on Him. What a reason to celebrate! Grosgrain ribbon (¼″) and free-form flower shapes in primary colors can be assembled easily for this colorful banner. Attach the ribbon streamers only at the flowers and allow them to hang freely, extending below the bottom of the banner.

Banner 34—Matthew 22:37

Jesus replied: "Love the Lord your God with all your heart and with all your soul and with all your mind." Matthew 22:37

Have you noticed how letters want to jump from the line and fit together more naturally? Let them! Let these heart shapes and abstract shapes do that too. In design, it's not necessary to illustrate every word of the text. Hearts offer endless possibilities to the designer and, in this case, still allow the meaning of "soul" and "mind" to remain clear.

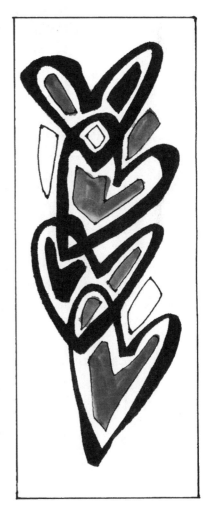

Banner 35—Matthew 22:39

You shall love your neighbor as yourself. Matthew 22:39 NRSV

Because the design elements in this three-part banner are more representational, you can make it more realistic by using sides of wooden pint baskets for the berry containers and clear plastic for the Mason jars. The plastic can be purchased by the foot at fabric and craft stores and can be sewn to the banner with bias tape on top. Calico fabric for the lids offers possibilities too. It also can remind us of the loving touches that God's people use as they share His bounty.

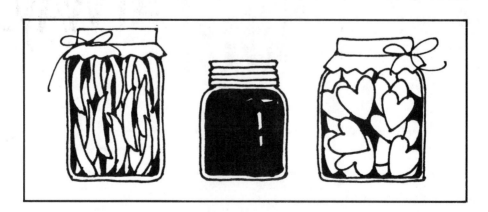

Banner 36 – Matthew 28:20

And surely I am with you always, to the very end of the age. Matthew 28:20

Christ's comforting promise to us is echoed by the large, all-encompassing shape of the design. This simple banner can be assembled quickly. Use fabric paint markers for the lines on the face and hands.

Banner 37—Matthew 28:20

And surely I am with you always, to the very end of the age.
Matthew 28:20

Eternity implies seeing through the present to what lies ahead. Using layers of semi-transparent organdy or other sheer fabric will help symbolize this. The construction creates a mystery with no beginning or ending, just as Christ's promise extends in both of time's directions. Metallic gold thread in a running stitch, as indicated by the dashed lines in the design, adds another dimension to the layered pieces. Embroidery or beads can complete the design.

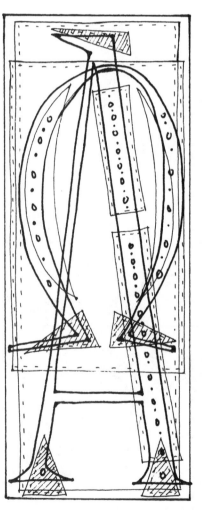

Banner 38—Luke 24:32

They said to each other, "Did not our hearts burn within us while He talked to us on the road, while He opened to us the scriptures?"
Luke 24:32 RSV

As He met with the disciples on their way to Emmaus, the risen Christ meets us "on our way"—to baseball practice, to work, on the freeway, on a jogging path. This banner celebrates those encounters. It can be assembled easily by using either a basic gluing or fusing technique. Use a fabric paint pen to complete the minimal outlining.

Banner 39—John 1:16

From His fullness we have all received, grace upon grace.
John 1:16 NRSV

That's how God's grace comes—in waves and layers. Sometimes, though, we only sense snippets of it. This design is a fast one. Perhaps another "grace" could be added and all three could be cut from a gradation of shades of one hue. Use your imagination for the snippets—colorful ticket stubs, postage stamps, campaign buttons, bottle caps—all examples of the too-many-to-count good things the Lord showers on us daily.

Banner 40—John 3:16

For God so loved the world that He gave His only Son, so that everyone who believes in Him may not perish but may have eternal life. John 3:16 NRSV

The sunrise message of this verse is depicted in the design's enormous sun, providing the dawn for a dark world. Shades of blue, purple, and green for the buildings can carry the idea effectively.

Banner 41 –
John 8:36

So if the Son sets you free, you will be free indeed.
John 8:36

The freedom Christ provides also can be celebrated with images of sparklers, fireworks, and Roman candles. Fabric paint and fabric paint markers in bright metallic colors can provide a striking contrast when used on a dark blue background. Complete the nighttime sky with star-shaped bangles. Metallic gold thread in a running stitch is an alternative way to create the numerous fine lines for the fireworks.

Banner 42—
John 10:27

My sheep hear My voice. I know them, and they follow Me. John 10:27 NRSV

The lines of this design indicate the not-always-straight paths of our less-than-perfect following of our Good Shepherd. But Jesus' voice is always there for us. The sheep's woolliness can be done in a variety of methods: black fabric paint pen, black yarn (or white yarn for a much more subtle effect), or figure-6 shapes cut from a contrasting fabric. For a tactile banner, use cotton balls!

Figure-6 shape for wool

Banner 43– John 10:27

My sheep hear My voice. I know them, and they follow Me. John 10:27 NRSV

The same verse as the previous banner, but this time in a diptych arrangement. Notice that Y-shapes make good tree trunks. Consider a variety of green calico prints for the trees and blue small prints for the river. Ideas for the lines on the sheep can be found with the notes for Banner 42.

Y-shapes

Banner 44—
John 14:6

Jesus answered, "I am the way and the truth and the life. No one comes to the Father except through Me." John 14:6

Designers and calligraphers love the configuration of the letters *E* and *T* that creates the ampersand—a fast way to write the word *and,* which is based on the Latin word *et.* The ampersand offers limitless possibilities because of its variety of lines. This time a cross has been worked into the ampersand to form the juncture of those things that Christ is—the way, the truth, the life. Notice too that some of the letters are fused to convey further the idea of wholeness. Try a black background, white letters, and a red ampersand and cross.

Banner 45—
John 15:5

I am the vine; you are the branches. If a man remains in Me and I in him, he will bear much fruit; apart from Me you can do nothing.
John 15:5

Block printing on fabric is an ancient art form and a practical way to create repeated images. The leaves and grapes on this banner can be applied in a variety of ways. Each method produces different printed qualities.

1. **Easiest**. Cut a leaf stencil from heavy paper and use a sponge to apply acrylic paint.

2. At an art supply store, purchase a linoleum block, cutting tools, block-printing ink, and a brayer. Using the leaf pattern on the banner (or a more intricate design of your own), cut a leaf design into the linoleum block. Ink it with the brayer, and print directly on the banner background. For the best results, place the background fabric on the floor and stand on the linoleum block. **Warning:** If this process intrigues you, block printing can be habit forming.

3. If the banner is small (perhaps a confirmation gift), the method in number 2 can be done with a potato. Slice a potato in half, and use a kitchen paring knife to cut a leaf design into the smooth surface. Ink the potato surface with acrylic ink and stamp away! For the grapes, use a carrot cut.

4. Use a real leaf as your "printing block." Experiment with both sides of the leaf to see which effect you like best. Try metallic inks on your leaf prints for a unique effect.

Banner 46—Acts 26:18

I will rescue you from your people and from the Gentiles—to whom I am sending you to open their eyes so that they may turn from darkness to light and from the power of Satan to God, so that they may receive forgiveness of sins and a place among those who are sanctified by faith in Me. Acts 26:18 NRSV

This banner trio contrasts life *without* Christ to life *in* Christ. It requires high contrast colors: black/white, midnight blue/light yellow, or violet/yellow. Use two colors (yellow and gold or white and yellow, for example) for the two-layered stars, moon, and sun rays. Allow the *t* in "light" to become a cross.

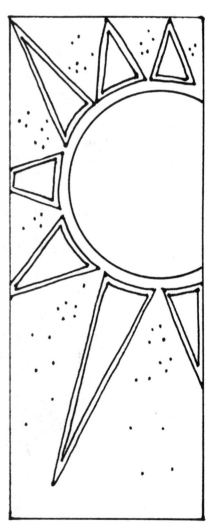

Banner 47—Romans 8:28

We know that in all things God works for good with those who love Him, those whom He has called according to His purpose. Romans 8:28 TEV

A variety of fabrics that are woven into a cross within a circle depicts how God is at work in our lives and how He holds everything together. (The fabrics could be reminders of events from your life if you use fabric from old clothing.) The design can be punctuated with buttons or beads.

Banner 48 — Romans 8:38

For I am convinced that neither death nor life, neither angels nor demons, neither the present nor the future, nor any powers, neither height nor depth, nor anything else in all creation, will be able to separate us from the love of God that is in Christ Jesus our Lord. Romans 8:38–39

The design symbolizes Paul's list of "large" things that pale in the face of God's love for us in Christ: heights, depths, powers, today, tomorrow, in fact, all of creation! Multicolored stars and multicolored rays from the center sphere create the "all of creation" look. Consider an analogous color scheme—blues and greens, perhaps (see page 15)—to show an integrated universe with God's love holding everything together.

Banner 49 – Romans 14:8

If we live, we live to the Lord; and if we die, we die to the Lord. So, whether we live or die, we belong to the Lord. Romans 14:8

The diagonal movement of the design signifies God's strong hold on us. The flower motif shows our growth in Him. Try a dark blue background with bright, light-colored flowers for this easily assembled banner.

WHETHER WE LIVE OR DIE

WE BELONG TO THE LORD

Banner 50—
1 Corinthians
13:13

*So faith, hope, love abide,
these three; but the greatest
of these is love.
1 Corinthians 13:13 RSV*

Because Christ's love lives in us, our responsive love for others spills out all over. In the construction of this banner, it's *all* in the positive/negative design—the heart cut-outs and the background fabric.

Banner 51 –
Galatians
2:20

I have been crucified with Christ and I no longer live, but Christ lives in me. The life I live in the body, I live by faith in the Son of God, who loved me and gave Himself for me. Galatians 2:20

When words or images "bleed," or run off the edge, a larger-than-life effect is created. When we die and are reborn in Christ through Baptism, the result is an immense event. Bright, high-contrast colors pull the big, bold image together with the big, bold message.

Banner 52 –
Philippians
1:4

In all my prayers for all of you, I always pray with joy. Philippians 1:4

The glow of joy can be depicted with the overlapping of semi-transparent organdy. Use gold metallic thread in a running stitch, as indicated by the dashed lines on the design, to hold the glowing shapes to the background. The angle of the tapers also enhances the joyful theme. A dark background color will allow the organdy layers to show.

Banner 53—Philippians 4:4

Rejoice in the Lord always; again I say, Rejoice. Philippians 4:4 NRSV

The flowing lines and white robes are meant to bring to mind baptism in the waters of the Jordan. Using a different bright primary color for each section of the line that flows through the figures will define the joy that is evident in Baptism and in Paul's joyful message to the Philippians. A small version of this could make a meaningful baptismal gift.

Banners 54 and 55—Philippians 2:10–11; 4:13

At the name of Jesus every knee should bow, in heaven and on earth and under the earth, and every tongue confess that Jesus Christ is Lord, to the glory of God the Father. Philippians 2:10–11

I can do all things through Him who strengthens me. Philippians 4:13 NRSV

The complementary themes of kneeling in humility before the Lord and being lifted up by His strength—both found in Paul's letter to the Philippians—form the themes for these companion banners. The two directions of the words echo the dual directions in which the Christian is called. These designs were made with brush strokes so consider painting directly on the banner backgrounds with a large round brush and acrylic paint. Outlining the shield and palm branches first with a pencil or fabric marker and using a heavy background fabric like canvas will make the painting easier.

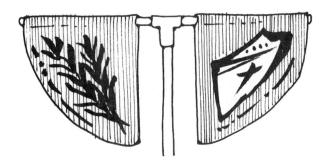

These banners can hang together, one on each side of the center pole for a standing banner. Or they can hang from the rafters in the opposite configuration.

I CAN DO ALL THINGS THROUGH CHRIST WHO S·T·R·E·N·G·T·H·E·N·S ME

Banner 56 – Colossians 1:19

For in Him all the fullness of God was pleased to dwell. Colossians 1:19 NRSV

The circle with the cross at its center depicts the God-and-man being of Christ described in Colossians 1:19 as well as in verse 17: "In Him all things hold together" (NRSV). A centered creation and a centered life in Christ are shown with a very busy circle of bright design elements in bright colors.

Banner 57 —
1 John 1:9

If we confess our sins, He is faithful and just and will forgive us our sins and purify us from all unrighteousness. 1 John 1:9

In this design the words of God's promise literally cover the words of confession, just as Jesus' blood covers our sins when we confess and receive His absolution. Two shades of the same hue might be used for this banner with the more intense shade on top.

Banner 58– Revelation 2:10

Be faithful, even to the point of death, and I will give you the crown of life. Revelation 2:10

This design is a reminder that, in the end, God makes everything fit: the dark times; the bright, shiny times; the infinite variety of events that shapes our lives. Through the gift of faith, God brings us safely to the crown of life. The crazy-quilt look of this banner needs a chain stitch (see page 27) to cover the edges of the shapes. A discarded necklace might see new life as beads for the finishing touch on this design.

COLOR WHEEL
(see pages 14–15)

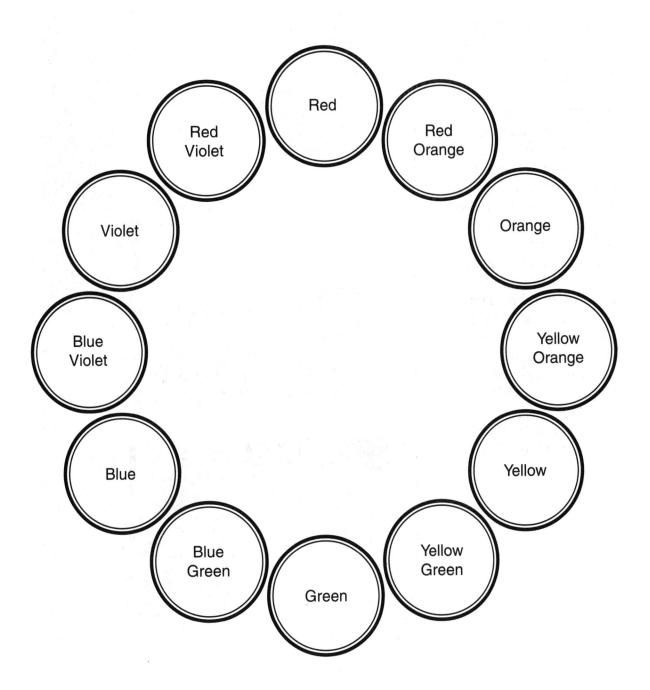

NOTES